THE CHRISTIAN COMFORT COMPANION

Chaplain Maceo Gray, Th.M
Annie P. Gray, MA

THE CHRISTIAN COMFORT COMPANION

Published by:
Hope Again Ministries Publishing
P. O. Box 481331
Kansas City, MO 64148
(816) 718-4441

Cover Painting: Barbara Burnett, The Shepherd Boy

ISBN: 1-929264-11-9

First person singular narratives refer to Chaplain
Maceo Gray.
Plural narratives refer to Chaplain Maceo Gray
and his wife, Annie P. Gray.

TABLE OF CONTENTS

ACKNOWLEDGMENTS

We are extremely grateful and thankful for the encouragement, insight, and contributions made by several people in the writing of this book. In particular, we are indebted to our daughter, Kathleen A. Smith, and her husband, Todd H. Smith, and my brother Brucy C. Gray, and his wife, Ethel P. Gray, for glorifying God through their personal losses.

We are also grateful to Dr. Dan Truitt, Dr. Victor Borden, Jeanette Littleton, and Mark Littleton for making suggestions, and critiquing manuscripts of the book. Their encouragement and insights were invaluable and deeply appreciated.

PROLOGUE OF GRIEF

Blessed be the God and Father of our Lord Jesus Christ, the Father of mercies and God of all comfort, who comforts us in all our tribulation, that we may be able to comfort those who are in any trouble, with the comfort with which we ourselves are comforted by God.
(2 Corinthians 1:3-4)

Concerning this thing I pleaded with the Lord three times that it might depart from me. And He said to me, "My grace is sufficient for you, for My strength is made perfect in weakness." Therefore, most gladly I will rather boast in my infirmities, that the power of Christ may rest upon me. **(2 Corinthians 12:8-9)**

These things I have spoken to you, that in Me you may have peace. In the world you will have tribulation, but be of good cheer, I have overcome the world. **(John 16:33)**

*T*he *Christian Comfort Companion* was written to help those of you who have suffered the death of a loved one recover from grief. We want to help you do this by helping you receive comfort from the God of all comfort, find God's grace to be sufficient, and experience the peace of God through Jesus Christ, our Lord.

The book is a handy companion, small enough for you to easily carry with you and frequently refer to during your grief recovery processes. *The Christian Comfort Companion* helps you understand the grieving processes. It also provides channels for God's intervention through twelve remedies called "Prescriptions of Grief Recovery."

Rev. Maceo Gray, as a Chaplain with Marketplace Ministries, provides comfort, compassion, and hope to many families suffering from the death of loved ones. However, he and his wife, Annie (Ann) P. Gray, wrote this book of comfort after experiencing two personal tragedies. Their daughter, Kathleen A. Smith, delivered a 20 week old still-born baby girl, Baby J. Within a few months of this tragedy, Maceo and Ann also suffered the unexpected death of their 27 year-old nephew, Anthony Nolan Gray. Through these tragedies, and other experiences, they developed the concepts and processes of *The Christian Comfort Companion* to help them personally experience God's comfort, grace, and peace in recovering from their grief. In accordance with 2 Corinthians 1:3-4, they want to comfort you as they have been comforted, so you, too, can hope again.

The Christian Comfort Companion is dedicated to Maceo and Ann Gray's daughter, Kathleen A. Smith, and her husband, Todd H. Smith; and to Chaplain Gray's brother, Brucy C. Gray, and his wife, Ethel P. Gray, in memory of their children. Both couples are finding God's comfort, grace, and peace to also be healing and sufficient.

PROBLEM OF GRIEF

One of the dictionary definitions for *grief* is: "emotional suffering caused by bereavement (death of a loved one)." This is the definition we will use in *The Christian Comfort Companion*. With this definition, we see that "grief" is natural because it results from experiencing a traumatic situation in our lives, such as a loved one's death. It is an emotional response to a catastrophic loss in our lives.

When our emotions suffer, we experience grief. Since grief is a natural reaction to loss, we should grieve or mourn. Preaching His Sermon on the Mount, Jesus said: *Blessed are those who mourn (grieve) for they shall be comforted (Matthew 5:4)*. The reason those who mourn are blessed is because God will comfort them. When we let ourselves be comforted by God, we experience a natural grieving process that Jesus says is a blessing. When we don't experience a natural grieving process, grief becomes overwhelming, and we may become stagnant, and never fully recover from our loved one's death.

The Christian Comfort Companion will help you "hope again" by redirecting your hope from yourself or others to the source of all of our hope, our Lord and Savior, Jesus Christ. If you do not have a relationship with Jesus Christ, you grieve without hope. But God can use your loved one's death to cause you to commit your life to Him and "hope again." Maybe previously your hope was in the very loved one who died. Now you can place your hope in Jesus Christ who overcame death. God physically brought Him back to life (resurrected) to never die again, after He was crucified on the cross. God loves you and knows exactly what you are going through. Right now you may not feel His love because your emotions are suffering from grief. But we want to encourage you to continue to read

3

through *The Christian Comfort Companion* and experience God's love.

As you journey through this book, if you begin to sense that you really don't know God but would like to know Him and be in a right relationship with Him, don't ignore it. God may be causing you to desire to know Him personally through faith and trust in Jesus Christ, His only Son. If this happens, simply stop and tell God in prayer that you know that you have not lived a perfect life and have fallen short of His holy requirement for us to do so. Tell Him you realize that when we fall short of His requirements, we sin, and need His forgiveness. Tell Him you believe Jesus Christ died for your shortcomings (sin) and you sincerely want Him to forgive you so you can be in a right relationship with Him.

Commit your life to God by trusting in Jesus Christ and what He has done for you through His death, burial and resurrection. Humbly ask Him to become the center of your life. Promise God that you will live the rest of your life for Him. You can read more information on how to enter a personal relationship with Jesus Christ in the "Postlude of Grief" section of this book. When you receive Jesus Christ as your Lord and Savior, you too can "hope again."

As believers in Jesus Christ, we place our faith and hope on what we know about Christ's victory over death through His resurrection. We depend upon His promise that when we die, we, too, will be resurrected like Him, and will live with Him forever. This basis allows us to successfully move through the natural process of grieving, although we may be tossed about as if we're riding a roller coaster. Grief doesn't have a specific pattern or time limit — it differs with each individual. There are no set standards for grief. But in spite of this, we can "hope again" because of our faith. By reading this book, may you find God's supernatural comfort to help you successfully move through the grieving processes.

PROCESSES OF GRIEF

The time of grief spent in one process is not the same for everyone. Also, one process may overlap another process. Some people may even question whether the identification of "grief processes" is of any practical value considering how overwhelming the phases of grief may be. C. S. Lewis, the English theologian, noted in *A Grief Observed* that grief is unpredictable, and one phase may jump over, coincide with, and merge with another. After the death of his wife, Joy, Lewis wrote:

> Tonight all the hells of young grief have opened again, the mad words, the bitter resentment, the fluttering in the stomach, the nightmare unreality, the wallowed-in tears. For in grief nothing "stays put." One keeps on emerging from a *phase*, but it always recurs. Round and round. Everything repeats. Am I going in circles, or dare I hope I am on a spiral? But if a spiral, am I going up or down it?[1]

When C. S. Lewis recorded these observations in his journal, he was suffering through the emotional phases of grief, although he, too, recognized that grief goes through distinct processes as well as phases. At that time, he saw grief as a period of circular motion or cycles. At times, you may experience the same feelings and see grief in terms of phases rather than processes.

The emotional swings are phases, but we have specifically chosen processes to define the complete movement of grief. The dictionary defines a process as:

---

[1]   C. S. Lewis, A Grief Observed (New York: Bantam Books, 1976), 66-67.

"A natural phenomenon marked by gradual changes that lead toward a particular result."

As you read *The Christian Comfort Companion*, we pray that the Holy Spirit will use the biblical truths you find here to heal your suffering emotions as you move through these three distinct grief recovery processes: *Resisting Reality, Readjusting to Reality, and Reattaining Reality.* When you complete the last process, you will have been comforted through the pain. You will have moved to the desired result of accepting your loved one's death and reestablishing your life toward "hope again" in Jesus Christ. Let's now look at the first process of grief, "Resisting Reality."

RESISTING REALITY

Shock

The shock phase is the beginning of the grieving process. For many people, the first day of grief begins like a normal day but ends in a way they could never have imagined. For others, death is expected. You may have had time to attempt to prepare for the inevitable, the death of your loved one.

When we were completing the final manuscript of this book, my mother-in-law died unexpectedly in her sleep at the age of 88 with no apparent serious sickness. Our day began as normal, but drastically changed when I received a voice mail page from Martha Nero, Ann's sister in Fort Worth, Texas. Her voice was broken as she stated: "Maceo, this is Martha, mother was found dead in her bed this morning and we are leaving now to go to Fairfield, Texas." I went to the college where Ann was teaching English as a Second Language (ESL) to international students. Nervously, without knowing how she would react, I waited outside the classroom to inform her of the news immediately after her class was over. When I told her, the shock was devastating although she made no physical outburst as we embraced each other. I could feel her heart beating extremely fast as she said, "I'm okay, lets go home now." Several of her students sensed something was wrong and expressed their condolences, using the best English that they could. The news of my mother-in-law's death was shocking because it was so unexpected. Everything seemed so unreal and distant as we prepared to travel to Texas.

When my mother died in the hospital at the age of 91 after being sick for quite some time, it wasn't totally unexpected. My brother, Dr. James Gray, called in the middle of the night and told us of her death. I had visited her at Baylor hospital earlier that day and could tell she was getting weaker. I had begun to prepare my mind for the inevitable. When the news came, I was still devastated and the emotional pain of the news seemed to have numbed by entire body for several days.

Shock is the *immediate emotional response* to a traumatic experience. Maybe the doctor came out of your loved one's hospital room and informed you of the death; or you received a telephone call in the middle of the night; or a relative, friend, or policeman came over to your house. Or maybe you were present when your loved one died. Whether you expected the death or not, you experienced some form of shock. Your mind may have wanted to simply shut down.

Some people immediately show a physical reaction such as collapsing, sobbing hysterically, experiencing shortness of breath, shaking or trembling, being unable to speak, or showing a verbal and physical outburst of anguish. When Brad, a young man in my Sunday school class, learned at the hospital that his wife had died, he had to be restrained by security as he hysterically beat the walls in anguish and despair.

However, others may not show any obvious physical reaction. They may respond unexpectedly, such as continuing to talk and behave as if they did not hear the news. Or they may seem disconnected from everyone, cold, unfriendly, and aloof. They may experience a sense of tunnel vision for days.

Regardless of your apparent response to the news of your loved one's death, you are in some form of shock. Don't be ashamed or afraid you are losing your mind. You probably could not predict your initial response to hearing about your loved one's death.

Shock is a normal process of grief and may last for several hours or days. It jolts us and may seem to be a time of sheer horror. But be encouraged, the immediate trauma of shock will gradually subside, especially when you feel the love and presence of God, the church, relatives, and friends. Your doctor may also prescribe some medication to help you get through this phase of grief so you can rest.

Denial

When I served as a chaplain at a bank in Dallas, a 27 year-old employee, who was married with two kids, suddenly became gravely ill. When the doctor told the family the young lady had no brain activity, they decided to disconnect life support, and she died. During the young mother's ordeal, her husband was in denial and couldn't accept the gravity of her condition. He would not visit the ICU area but stayed in the visitors' lounge. As her condition continued to deteriorate, I would give him a status report. Each time, he would ask me if what was happening was real. After she died, I informed him of her death and I will never forget his words: "No, Maceo, tell me it isn't true." Although he agreed with family members to disconnect life support, initially, he just couldn't accept her death.

The "denial phase" often merges with the "shock phase." You hear the words, but your mind automatically wants to protect you, so you reject what you hear. "It just can't be true. Everything was going so well." You may have just planned to do some small things with your loved one ... walking in the park after dinner, shopping together, or going to see your son start his first varsity game. Maybe you had been saving money to take that big vacation. So "This can't be happening," you reason. He or she was the one you had lived for, your soul mate, the parent you so admired, or that precious child who would carry on the family business, or be the first pastor or doctor in the family.

"Am I dreaming?" "Is this a nightmare?" It just can't be true. "Will someone please wake me up?" you wonder. But unfortunately, you are awake. You may list reasons why this can't be happening. The pregnancy was going so well, he was such a good swimmer, she drove so carefully, he was the picture of health, she just wouldn't take her own life, and the doctor said he was getting better, but I thought her cancer had gone into remission. Your mind can't accept the facts and therefore, you begin to deny the reality of the facts. Even if you expected the inevitable, you may still be in denial when it actually occurs.

Denial is a prevalent phase of the "Resisting Reality" process. This phase may last even beyond the funeral, but in most cases, the funeral tends to break down the denial phase of grief. The funeral is important to grief recovery because it usually forces the mind to begin to accept the reality of the death. Your tendency to speak of the deceased in present and future tenses begins to decline after the funeral. As much as it hurts, you must not continue to deny your loved one's death. This is a critical step in being able to experience God's comfort, grace, and peace as you move into the second grief recovery process of "Readjusting to Reality."

READJUSTING TO REALITY

When you move into this process, you have taken a gigantic step toward grief recovery. Although your emotions are still suffering, your mind has begun to accept the reality of your loved one's death. You may still go through moments or phases in which your emotions want you to go back to resisting reality. But be encouraged that you are making progress, and realize that those moments of despair are normal.

Some people say the funeral allows you to put closure to the death, but it doesn't. It does usually force the mind to begin accepting the reality of the death. When this occurs, you and others will recognize it. You may begin to make adjustments in your life, although this is an extremely painful step. Try not to make any major decisions at this time, such as financial investments, entering new long-term relationships, selling your home, or quitting your job. You are still grieving and your emotions are suffering, so your ability to make good decisions is probably diminished.

As we readjust to reality after a death, we feel and express many emotions. Let's analyze these emotions by looking at the death of Lazarus of Bethany, and noting how his sisters, Mary and Martha, responded to Jesus. In John 11:19-37, we see these women express several different types of emotions in their encounters with Jesus.

And many of the Jews had joined the women around
Martha and Mary, To comfort them concerning
their brother[his death].
Now Martha, as soon as she heard that Jesus was coming,
went and met Him, but Mary was sitting in the house.
Now Martha said to Jesus, "Lord, if you had been here,
my brother would not have died.
But even now I know that whatever You ask of God,
God will give You."

Jesus said to her, "Your brother will rise again."
Martha said to Him, "I know that he will rise again in the
resurrection at the last day."
Jesus said to her, "I am the resurrection and the life.
He who believes in Me, though he may die, he shall live.
And whoever lives and believes in Me shall never die.
Do you believe this?"
She said to Him, "Yes Lord, I believe that You are the
Christ, the Son of God, who is to come into the world."
And when she had said these things, she went her way and
secretly called Mary, her sister, saying,
"The Teacher has come and is calling for you."
As soon as she heard that,
she arose quickly and came to Him.
Now Jesus had not yet come into the town,
but was in the place where Martha met Him.
Then the Jews who were with her in the house, and
comforting her when they saw that Mary rose up quickly
and went out followed her saying,
"She is going to the tomb to weep there."
Then, when Mary came where Jesus was, and saw Him, she
fell down at His feet, saying to Him, "Lord, if You had been
here, my brother would not have died."
Therefore, when Jesus saw her weeping,
and the Jews who came with her weeping,
He groaned in the spirit and was troubled.
And He said, "Where have you laid him?"
They said to Him, "Lord come and see."
Jesus wept.
Then the Jews said, "See how He loved him!"
And some of them said, "Could not this Man, who opened
the eyes of the blind, also have kept this man from dying?"

Anger & Blame

As we see in the narrative of Lazarus' death, Mary and Martha lit into Jesus when he arrived. Although Jesus was the family's good friend, who occasionally stayed with them when he was in the area, both Martha and Mary were somewhat angry with Him. They blamed Lazarus' death on Him. Jesus had deliberately delayed his trip to Bethany by two days, when he heard that Lazarus was sick (John 11:6-7).

Both Martha and Mary made the same accusatory statement to Jesus, "Lord, if you had been here, my brother would not have died." In that one statement, we see both anger and blame. So if you get angry and blame God it does not mean you have completely lost your faith. You may also be angry with the doctor for not responding faster and blame him for the death. When you called 911, maybe it seemed to have taken all day for the ambulance to arrive, and you are angry with the ambulance attendants, and blame them for the death. Maybe you are angry with yourself for not coming home sooner or for not forcing your loved one to seek medical help. These natural emotions reflect some progress in the grief recovery processes. The expressions of anger and blame indicate that you have accepted the reality of the death.

Consider this contemporary example of anger and blame:

When Harry Ramos died while trying to help a stranger named Victor escape from the burning World Trade Center, the world turned him into a hero. His wife, Migdalia, was angry. She was angry at herself, angry at Victor, angry at all the wives whose husbands had come home safely and even angry at her husband. Still mourning the death of her mother just 10 days earlier, she was left alone with two small children, a half-built house, a flood

15

of bills and questions that would not go away about how her husband had put a stranger ahead of his family.[2]

Although Migdalia was angry with just about everyone, including herself, this was a normal phase of her grief recovery. It is important not to hide or ignore the anger and desire to blame someone, but admit that work is needed in this area. Ask God to help you through it using the "Prescriptions of Grief Recovery" as an aid — especially the "Prescription of Pardoning."

Crying

In the narrative of Lazarus' death, we also see grief expressed through crying. In the process of "Readjusting to Reality," crying is an emotional outlet. Although Lazarus had been buried, his sisters and friends were still crying over his death. Besides their tears, motivated by His love for Lazarus and His compassion for their pain, *Jesus wept*, even though He knew He would resurrect Lazarus from the dead (John 11:35).

If Jesus cried at the death of Lazarus, even knowing He would resurrect him, why should you try to keep from crying? If you are still crying at times, don't be discouraged. You are making progress and crying is a normal part of grieving. Some people discourage crying. But refusing to cry may actually impede your successful passage through the grief recovery processes.

If you are progressing through the grief recovery processes satisfactorily, your frequency of crying should decrease. You may find that your crying spells usually occur in certain situations or times, such as holidays, your loved one's birthday, or other events that vividly remind

---

[2] Mary Williams Walsh, War Stories (The Kansas City Star Newspaper, December 18, 2001), E3.

you of your loved one. The "Prescription of Periodic Reconciliation" section of this book provides aids to help you adjust to these memories and times.

Wavering Faith

Being a Christian does not mean that during times of grief, we won't begin to question what we know is true concerning the death of our loved one who was also a Christian. Some grieving people want to be assured of what heaven is like while others can't seem to understand why God would let their loved one die. When I was a chaplain at a Dallas bank, a dedicated Christian lady's husband died unexpectedly. For several months she questioned why God had let her husband die. She also raised many questions concerning proof of eternal life. After a while, she began to reaffirm her faith in Christ and found the assurance that her husband was in His presence.

Our faith may become paralyzed and overwhelmed by grief as we try to readjust to reality. As we continue to look at the narrative of Lazarus' death, we see a real switch between Mary and Martha in their outward expressions of faith.

Before Lazarus' death, Mary worshipped at Jesus' feet while Martha complained to Jesus that Mary was not helping with the household chores. Jesus slightly scolded Martha, by pointing out that she was worried about too many unnecessary things. He commended Mary for focusing on what was best and necessary (Luke 10:38-42). Jesus seemed to be praising Mary for her expression of faith in Him.

However, after Lazarus' death, Martha, not Mary, ran to meet Jesus before He arrived at the house. Martha, not Mary, told Jesus that she believed that whatever He asked God for, God would give to Him (John 11:22). Martha, not Mary, professed that she believed Jesus was the Christ, the Son of God, who had come into the world

(John 11:27). Where was Mary during this time? She was in the house, overwhelmed with grief, as her friends tried to comfort her (John 11:31). Martha demonstrated her faith by running to meet the Source of all hope, while Mary's grief paralyzed her efforts to readjust to reality.

Be aware that grief may paralyze your faith as you try to readjust to reality. This does not mean your faith is not genuine. Your faith may be tested during grief, but don't despair. Hang on to what you believe and know about God. Your mind may begin to ask questions similar to these:

- If God is a good God, and I belong to Him, why did this happen?
- Where is God?
- What did we do to deserve this?
- Does God really love me?
- As faithful as I have been in serving God, why did He allow this to happen to me?
- Is God really in control and sovereign over everything?

After Lazarus died, some of the friends and neighbors who had come to comfort Martha and Mary asked a penetrating question: *Could not this Man, who opened the eyes of the blind, also have kept this man from dying (John 11:37)?* We are not sure if these others were true believers in Jesus Christ, but they did acknowledge His supernatural power. The answer to their question is a resounding *YES*. Jesus could have kept Lazarus from dying, but death occurs for many reasons. Sometimes it is meant to glorify God (John 11:4).

As a metaphoric example, we see life with unaided eyes, but God sees life looking through an infinitely powered telescope because He is life. In other words, we tend to look at life with a temporal material perspective, but God looks at life with an eternal, immaterial perspective.

Before Lazarus' death, Martha primarily focused on a temporal, material perspective — taking care of the household chores. Jesus wanted her to focus with an eternal, immaterial perspective, which she successfully did after Lazarus' death.

We do not always know why things occur in our lives, but a time will come when we will know. When we come into God's presence, we will understand. God tells us that His thoughts and ways are much higher than ours:

> *For my thoughts are not your thoughts,*
> *Nor are you ways My ways, says*
> *the LORD.*
> *"For as the heavens are higher than the earth,*
> *So are My ways higher than your ways,*
> *And My thoughts than your thoughts.* (Isaiah 55:8-9)

We want to encourage you to rest on God's truth, His infallible Word. Trust Him to be a God Who can do no wrong and Who dearly loves you.

REATTAINING REALITY

It took about three years for me to actually reach this point in grief recovery when my father died, followed the next year by my mother's death. It may take you more or less time. I reached a point when the frequency, duration, and height of my emotional pain subsided. I now have a completely new outlook on life and a deeper and closer walk with the Lord without my parents. I don't have any regrets, although I do miss my parents. I am thankful for their longevity and for the legacy and values they left. I have accepted their deaths and truly believe they are in Christ's presence with joy everlasting.

The pinnacle of grief recovery is having reached the highest mountain, "Reattaining Reality" so you can hope again. You reach this mountain when you finally accept your loved one's death without bitterness, hatred, anger, guilt, and regrets, and you have peace with God. You have discovered God's grace was truly sufficient for you as His strength was made perfect in your weakness of grief. Your emotions are no longer suffering, and you now have a completely new outlook on life. Your new reality is life without your loved one.

This does not mean you have forgotten about your loved one. It simply means you have come to accept what has happened, and that God has given you comfort, grace, and peace, enabling you to continue life with new meaning and purpose even though your loved one is not with you. It also doesn't mean that you no longer miss your loved one.

When, after the death of a loved one, we can truly worship, praise, and bless God, with all of our heart, soul, and mind, and have peace with Him, and a new meaning and purpose in life, we have reattained reality.

Let's look at an example of a man who probably suffered more than anyone else, except Jesus Christ, and see how he responded to reattaining reality. We know Job's suffering was not caused by sin or anything that he had done because God bragged on him to Satan, saying: *"There is none like him on the earth, a blameless and upright man, who fears God and shuns evil"* (Job 1:8). Yet Job suffered the loss of all of his material possessions, as well as the death of his ten children. When he learned of his children's deaths, Job's response is interesting (Job 1:20-22):

> *Then Job arose, tore his robe, and shaved his head;*
> *and he fell to the ground and worshipped.*
> *And he said:*
> *"Naked I came from my mother's womb,*
> *And naked shall I return there.*
> *The LORD gave, and the LORD has taken away.*
> *Blessed be the name of the LORD."*
> *In all of this Job did not sin*
> *nor charge God with wrong."*

Maybe you have a lot in common with Job. You feel the pain of your suffering to the same degree as Job did. You feel your loved one's death was just not right and you did not deserve this distress. You have suffered almost unbearable pain, but you have the potential of reaching the "Reattaining Reality" process and eventually being able to respond as Job did. Job came to accept the death of his children, and could worship and bless God. What tremendous faith! Through his personal suffering, Job was able to glorify God.

You may not reach this point in a few months or a year or two. But that is the goal. Regardless of how long it takes you to arrive, keep working through the power of the Holy Spirit as you are aided by the "Prescriptions of Grief Recovery" section of this book. The twelve prescriptions are prescribed remedies we have found to be extremely helpful in overcoming grief. We present them to you through personal experiences and observations. May you find God's comfort, grace, and peace as you fully apply the remedies in the "Prescriptions of Grief Recovery" process.

PRESCRIPTIONS OF
GRIEF RECOVERY

Grief is unpredictable and has no set pattern for how a person rebounds from it. However, with that said, we believe God has shown us some prescriptions that should facilitate your recovery. These have come over the years, as we have closely examined God's Word and studied how God has helped us and others go through grief. Let's look at the first of twelve prescriptions, "Prescription of Presence."

PRESCRIPTION OF PRESENCE

We feel alone when we hear of a loved one's death, although we may be with many others. When I learned of the death of our nephew, Anthony Nolan Gray, Ann and I were hosting a dinner for about 20 Marketplace Ministries' chaplains and prospective chaplains. They had come to Kansas City to attend a Chaplain Training School taught by Dr. Dan Truitt. The occasion was joyous as we enjoyed fellowship.

During this time, the telephone rang. When I answered it, I knew something terrible had happened. My sister, Mary Marshall Batts, of Fort Worth, Tex., was on the line. I could hardly hear her words because she was sobbing and because of the noise from the dinner. But I did hear: "Maceo, Anthony, was found dead."

As I raced upstairs to another phone, I wondered which Anthony she meant — her four year-old grandson or our 27 year-old nephew. She only knew the police had notified my brother within the hour that our nephew had been found dead in his apartment. I could hear laughter from those enjoying the dinner and fellowship, but I still felt alone. I went to the bedroom and prayed, because I knew I was not alone, God was with me.

Presence of God
Psalm 23:4 clearly shows us that the Lord is with us during times of grief:

> *Yea, though I walk through the valley*
> *of the shadow of death,*
> *I will fear no evil; for You are with me;*
> *Your rod and Your staff, they comfort me.*

We also find comfort in God's presence in Isaiah
> *Fear not, for I am with you;*
> *Be not dismayed, for I am your God.*

27

I will strengthen you. Yes, I will help you.
I will uphold you with My righteous right hand.

As I prayed, I sensed God's comforting right hand upon my shoulder and my spirit felt His presence and love. I was not alone, nor did I feel that my brother and family were alone. God was present to strengthen and help us. We were to depend upon His strength to see us through this tragedy.

Just as I sensed God's comfort as I called out to Him, you too can receive the same strength during your time of recovery. Initially, you may be so overwhelmed with grief that you don't feel God's presence. But He is ever with you in your time of trouble. He has promised to be there, to strengthen you, to help you, and to uphold you during your grief. The Holy Spirit indwells every believer and is therefore present with you at all times. God gives you supernatural comfort through the indwelling Holy Spirit.

God is also present as we read His Word, the Holy Bible. Although you may not initially feel like reading, God's Word is the primary way He speaks to us today. You will experience God's presence through reading His Word. We have included in this chapter a "Prescription of Promises" and a "Prescription of Poetry." Reading these prescriptions is an excellent way to get into God's Word during your most difficult time. Read God's promises to you and reflect upon them. In the Old Testament, Hebrew poetry expressed the emotions of God's people in the form of praise, worship, thanks-giving and as they endured suffering and painful experiences. We have selected poetry from the Psalms and Lamentations to help you overcome your suffering.

Not only do we sense God's presence by praying and through the reading of His Word, we are also comforted and sense His presence through the "presence of people."

Presence of People
Presence of the Body of Christ
God uses the body of Christ, the church, to minister to those who are grieving. Isaiah 61: 1-2 clearly reveals the calling of God's anointed Servant to heal the brokenhearted and to comfort those who mourn.

The Spirit of the Lord God is upon Me,
*Because the L*ORD *has anointed Me*
To preach good tidings to the poor;
He has sent Me to heal the brokenhearted,
To proclaim liberty to the captives,
And the opening of the prison to those who are bound;
*To proclaim the acceptable year of the L*ORD*.*
And the day of vengeance of our God;
To comfort all who mourn.

The anointed Servant was a prophecy of Christ, fulfilled in Luke 4:18-22. Today, the call applies to Christ's church and is administered through the Holy Spirit by His representatives, the pastor, and the local body of Christ. We have seen and experienced an excellent portrayal of this after the death of our nephew, Anthony Nolan Gray.

When we flew to Dallas, we were amazed at the outpouring of love and comfort from Pastor Mary Beth Crouch and the members of Trinity United Methodist Church in Duncanville, Tex. The pastor visited the home several times to pray with and encourage the family. Many members stopped by to express their genuine love and concern.

We were indeed blessed and ministered to by Pastor Crouch as she worked with us in making funeral arrangements and preparing the service. She sincerely wanted to meet the family's wishes and showed a genuine concern for us. I was pleased to participate in the services with her, and to be comforted from her special message from God. Many church members brought food and were available to do whatever the family needed. The church didn't leave anything undone, even providing a house sitter during the funeral.

God has designed the local church to fulfill this role in comforting and ministering to grieving families. Trinity United Methodist Church beautifully demonstrated this role. Our family was indeed comforted by their ministry.

Presence of Relatives, Friends & Others

When a loved one dies, the presence of relatives, and friends often provides comfort. We see this example in John 11:19:

> *And many of the Jews had joined the women around*
> *Martha and Mary, to comfort them*
> *concerning their brother [his death].*

We knew that my brother, Brucy, and his wife, Ethel, would have very quick support by family members who live in Dallas. But God had also arranged for our oldest brother and his wife, Wilmer and Irene, to be visiting in the home when the police brought the news of Anthony's death. Relatives from all over the United States and Puerto Rico came to Dallas. Many friends of the family also joined us.

We were also comforted as Marketplace Ministries' Director of Development, Larry Ramsey, and his wife, Mary, attended the funeral. The Founder and President of Marketplace Ministries, Gil Stricklin, and the entire staff offered comfort with phone calls and cards.

The "Prescription of Presence" is essential to your grieving process. Regardless of the situation surrounding a loved one's death, you should accept the outpouring love, concern, and comfort provided by the presence of the body of Christ, relatives, friends, and others. This is one of the many ways God extends His grace to grievers.

PRESCRIPTION OF PRECIOUS TEARS

Our tears are precious to God as expressed in Psalm 56:8:

You number my wanderings;
Put my tears into Your bottle;
Are they not in Your book?

God stores each tear drop in a bottle and keeps each one in His eternal record. Of course, this is a figurative way of assuring us that God notices our tears and knows about our suffering. What an encouragement to know that our tears are not expressions of useless, hopeless frustration. Our omniscient (all-knowing) God knows and cares about each tear we shed. He has designed us uniquely and given us an acceptable way to express our grief.

So remember that crying is an acceptable and essential act to help you recover from grief. People may discourage you from crying, but remember that Jesus wept at His friend Lazarus's grave (John 11:35) and that God considers your tears precious enough to catch each one and store it in His bottle and record it in His eternal book. He not only knows, but He keeps a record of the amount of suffering we experience. *God will never allow us to suffer more than His grace will allow us to handle.* So when you cry, you are not wasting time or tears because they are precious to God.

Our culture tends to indicate that it is acceptable for women and children to cry, but not for men. This is not correct. Crying gives us a way to release emotional suffering. Otherwise it may build up within us. When our emotions build and are not released, they may show through seemingly unrelated symptoms, such as inability to concentrate, restlessness, lack of patience, anger, and physical illnesses such as stomach aches, nervousness, indigestion, high blood pressure, and other ailments.

You may not realize the cause of some of the symptoms. You may believe you have completely recovered from a loved one's death. This happened to me when my parents died. My father and mother died within a year of each other at the ages of 89 and 91. My father died the same year I took early retirement from AlliedSignal to enter full-time ministry, although I'd yielded to God's call five years earlier. I was in my first year at Dallas Theological Seminary when my mother died. I felt I needed to be strong for my family and never fully released my grief through the "Prescription of Precious Tears." I had experienced several changes in a year ... my father's death, retirement, seminary, and my mother's death.

Grief comes and goes in phases. During a Bible study and prayer time in our local church, Sacred Trust Evangelical Church, in Dallas, I experienced a phase of grief I had not experienced before. I had exhibited some symptoms of unreleased grief, but did not know the cause. The tears began to flow and I didn't know how to stop them. As I expressed the hurt I was feeling over my parents' death, Pastor Elliott Greene, my wife, and other members of the church comforted me and prayed for me. They let me fully express my grief through precious tears. This occurred several years ago and I will always remember it as the threshold that allowed me to move through the grieving processes.

The "Prescription of Precious Tears" is another vital part of successfully moving through the grieving processes. We have attempted to remove the stigma of crying and to give you the biblical perspective of this expression of grief. May your precious tears be as acceptable to you as they are to God, in enabling you to experience His intervening comfort, grace, and peace.

PRESCRIPTION OF PRAYERS

God promises to answer us when we cry out to Him as He has expressed in Isaiah 58:9:

Then you shall call, and the LORD will answer;
You shall cry, and He will say, "Here I am."

And again in Psalm 55:22, we find:

Cast your burden on the LORD,
And He shall sustain you;
He shall never permit the righteous to
be moved.

As believers in Jesus Christ, we have access through His shed blood to go directly to the throne of grace as expressed in Hebrews 4:15-16:

For we do not have a High Priest
who cannot sympathize with our weaknesses,
but was in all points tempted as we are
yet without sin.
Let us therefore come boldly to the
throne of grace that we may obtain
mercy and find grace to help in time of need.

We have a compassionate High Priest in Jesus Christ who offers us mercy and forgiveness. High Priest means that He represents us to God the Father and acts as our go-between (mediator) to God enabling us to know God the Father. He suffers with us in our weaknesses and wants us to come to God boldly to find mercy and grace when we are tempted to sin. I am sure He also wants us to come boldly to God to find grace when our time of need is not temptation, but when we mourn over the death of a loved one. Isn't that comforting? We can go to the God of this universe with our prayers because of our compassionate High Priest, Jesus Christ. God hears us and has promised to help. What a marvelous treasure we have, especially during our time of grief.

Not only has God promised to hear our prayers, but He has also encouraged us to pray for one another, and He will also answer those prayers. Therefore, we should pray and be open to having others pray for us during the grief recovery processes. The "Prescription of Prayers," personal and intercessory, is a vital phase of grief recovery.

Personal Prayers

We are promised mercy and grace to help us during our time of grief when we go to the throne of grace. We are encouraged to go to the throne of grace with confidence because our High Priest, Jesus Christ, sits at God's right hand interceding for us. We don't have to be ashamed or afraid, and we can express all of our emotional pain to God. He offers us *mercy,* which means regardless of the anger or hurt we express, God will sympathize and not respond vindictively. We will also receive *grace* ,which is favor we don't deserve. Grace is God's demonstration of His loyal love when He enables us to hope again. His grace helps us carry on when we want to quit.

We don't have to do anything to receive this grace — He gives it to us because He loves us. His grace will enable us to successfully go through this devastating time. God promises to walk with us and provide everything we need to get through our loss.

Personal prayers helped us experience God's presence when our daughter, Kathleen, told us about a problem with her pregnancy. I was in the office when I received her call. When I answered the phone, I immediately detected that something was wrong. She was calm but serious when she said, "Daddy, Todd and I are at the doctor's office and we have a problem. The doctor cannot detect the baby's heartbeat, and she believes the baby is dead. Can you and Mom meet us at Saint Joseph Hospital?"

The morning had started so wonderfully, but now everything had changed. I didn't have time to reflect on the full impact of Kathleen's words, and didn't know if the doctor's assessment was true. But I knew God knew, so I immediately went to Him in prayer. I asked God to give us His grace to accept the outcome, and to be able to provide comfort and support to help the family go through this crisis. God's presence was personal and I sensed it through my prayers.

On some occasions, time seems to speed up when we face a crisis and other times it seems to slow down. Everything was happening so fast. I needed to tell Ann about the situation but couldn't reach her by phone. I met Kathleen and Todd at the hospital, and the doctor confirmed that "Baby J" did not have a heartbeat. Then I went to Ann's college class where she was teaching. We rushed back to the hospital where we prayed and comforted each other while the doctor induced labor.

You may want to pray, but not be able to during the initial phases of grief. Your emotions may swing up and down as you experience disappointment, anguish, fear, anger loneliness, desperation, and helplessness. Especially during this time you will find God's comfort through intercessory prayers.

Intercessory Prayers

James 5:16 encourages us to pray for one another to be healed by God. We are also told that praying for one another is not a waste of time, but a powerful operation.

*Confess your trespasses to one another,
and pray for one another, that you may be
healed. The effective, fervent prayer of a
righteous man avails much.*

Although the context probably refers to being healed from a physical sickness, God is ultimately the source of all healing — including emotional suffering. He may use doctors or other means, but He is the ultimate Source. Isn't it wonderful that when we are suffering so much that we can't pray, we can have faith that the prayers of other godly believers will help us move through the grieving processes so we may experience God's comfort, grace, and peace? Therefore, when our emotions are suffering as we experience grief, we should be open to intercessory prayers.

When we were at the hospital waiting for the stillbirth of Baby J, we sensed God's comfort through the prayers of members of our church, Red Bridge Baptist Church, pastored by Dr. Vic Borden, and Todd and Kathleen's church, Canaan Christian Fellowship, pastored by Todd's father, Rev. Andrew Smith. We were also comforted by the Holy Spirit through the intercessory prayers of the staff of Marketplace Ministries.

Personal prayers and intercessory prayers are not based on blind faith, but on God's promises to meet our needs in times of trouble. Let's now focus on these promises to help you successfully move through the grief processes by being reminded of God's assurances to you during your time of need.

PRESCRIPTION OF PROMISES

As we waited at St. Joseph Hospital for the Baby J's stillbirth, we had to rely upon what we knew about God to help us through the situation. We knew Baby J would be stillborn, and time seemed to have slowed considerably as we counted the minutes. We noticed the happy and proud fathers, grandparents, and other relatives as they learned the good news about new additions to their families. This wait was so different from our experiences during the births of our four other grandchildren. It was especially difficult.

Besides praying, we reflected on God's character and His promises to us. We found His promises to be extremely comforting, and want to share them with you. They helped us and sustained us through this time of grief. May you also find comfort by meditating on God's promises as you go through the grief processes.

Promise of God's Everlasting Love

For I am persuaded that neither death nor life,
nor angels nor principalities nor powers,
nor things present nor things to come,
nor height nor depth, nor any other
created thing, shall be able to separate us
from the love of God which is in Christ
our Lord. (Romans 8:38-39)

For God so loved the world that He gave
His only begotten Son, that whoever
believes in Him should not perish but
have everlasting life. (John 3:16)

Promise of God's Companionship

I will not leave you orphans
I will come to you. (John 14:18)

Promise of God's Help

God is our refuge and strength,
a very present help in trouble. (Psalm 46:1)

Why art you cast down, O my soul?
And why are you disquieted within me?
Hope in God: For I shall yet praise
Him. The help of my countenance,
and my God. (Psalm 42:11)

For He has not despised nor abhorred the
affliction of the afflicted; Nor has He
hidden His face from Him; But when He cried
to Him, He heard. (Psalm 22:24)

Promise of God's Comfort

Blessed be the God and Father of our
Lord Jesus Christ, the Father of mercies
and God of all comfort,
who comforts us in all our tribulations,
that we may be able to comfort those
who are in any trouble, with the comfort
with which we ourselves are comforted
by God. (2 Corinthians 1:3- 4)

But I do not want you to be ignorant,
brethren concerning those who have
fallen asleep[died], lest you sorrow as others
who have no hope.
For if we believe that Jesus died and
rose again, even so God will bring with
Him those who sleep in Jesus.
For the Lord Himself will descend from
heaven with a shout, with the voice of an
archangel, and with the trumpet of God.
And the dead in Christ will rise first.

Then we who are alive and remain shall be caught up together with them in the clouds to meet the Lord in the air. And thus we shall always be with the Lord. Therefore comfort one another with these words. (1 Thessalonians 4:13-18)

"And God will wipe away every tear from their eyes; there shall be no more death, nor sorrow, nor crying. There shall be no more pain, for the former things have passed away." (Revelation 21:4)

God's promises are true. Even though you may not understand why your loved one died, you can claim God's promises to help you move through the grief processes.

Most people move from the "Resistance to Reality" process to the "Readjusting to Reality" process after the funeral. This important function of parting enables you to overcome the denial phase. May you find the "Prescription of Parting" to be a pivotal point in grief recovery.

PRESCRIPTION OF PARTING

"George, come back, please don't leave me.
George, please come back. Please don't take him away!"
Though 44 years have passed, I still remember these chilling words as the funeral director came to the South Dallas home to take George's body to the church for the funeral services. George, a Lincoln High School senior who lived across the street from my family when I was a sophomore in high school, had accidentally killed himself while playing Russian Roulette.

George was his parents' only son, and they took his death especially hard. George's mother cried out her anguish as she was stuck in the "Resistance to Reality" process. As long as the body was in the home, she could hold on to him and resist the reality of his death.

The funeral is an important aspect of grief recovery because it helps us accept our loved one's death. It is an act of parting, physically separating the deceased loved one from those left behind. Luke 7:11-15 shows us that the funeral and procession played a vital part in helping people readjust to death during the time of Christ.

> Now it happened, the day after, that He [Jesus]
> went into a city called Nain; and many of His
> disciples went with Him, and a large crowd.
> And when He came near the gate of the city, behold,
> a dead man was being carried out, the only son of
> his mother, and she was a widow. And a large
> crowd from the city was with her.
> When the Lord saw her, He had compassion on her
> and said to her,
> "Do not weep."
> Then He came and touched the open coffin, and
> those who carried him stood still.
> And He said, "Young man, I say to you, arise."

43

So he who was dead sat up and began to speak.
And He presented him to
his mother.

We see in this text that a large crowd was following the widowed mother as she accompanied her son's body in a funeral procession. Then Jesus intervened. He told the grieving mother not to weep, because He knew He would raise her son from the dead. He was not indicating that crying was not good, but simply that soon she would not have anything to weep about.

Jesus had compassion on this mother, and He has the same compassion on us. He promises to also raise from the dead those who have trusted in Him. Therefore, we should not grieve as those who have no hope. Believers who die in Christ face a physical parting. However, we also have a promise of a physical resurrection with a glorified perfect body to reside with Him forever. So parting is only temporary, as we see in 1 Thessalonians 4: 13-16.

But I do not want you to be ignorant, brethren,
concerning those who have fallen asleep [died],
lest you sorrow as others who have no hope.
For if we believe that Jesus died and rose again,
even so God will bring with Him those who sleep in Jesus.
For this we say to you by the word of the Lord,
that we who are alive and
remain until the coming of the Lord will by no
means precede those who are asleep.
For the Lord Himself will descend from heaven with
a shout, with the voice of an archangel and with the
trumpet of God and the dead in Christ will rise first.

Our hope is in Christ and His promise to resurrect our loved one who died as a believer in Him. This hope enables us to see death as a threshold to eternal life with Jesus Christ our Lord.

Funeral directors, pastors, or chaplains can be very helpful to the family in deciding the funeral details. Their services are designed to ease your burden and to help you find comfort by showing the love you had for your loved one in the personal details of the funeral arrangements. The funeral can be traditional in a local church, a graveside ceremony, or a memorial, based upon your desires and the availability and condition of the body. The parting funeral service should be performed to help the family move from the "Resistance to Reality" process to the "Readjusting to Reality" process.

PRESCRIPTION OF POETRY

The books of poetry in the Old Testament include the Psalms and Lamentations. These books expressed the Israelites' emotions as they dealt with suffering, pain, death, and the joys of praising, thanking, and worshiping God Almighty. We have chosen Scriptures from these books to share with you because we found them to be extremely beneficial to us in the grief recovery processes. We suggest that you read and meditate on these special poetic scriptures to let God's supernatural comfort, grace, and peace minister to you through the Holy Spirit.

The LORD Is my shepherd
I shall not want.
He makes me to lie down in green
pastures;
He leads me besides the still waters.
He restores my soul;
He leads me in the paths of
righteousness
For His name's sake.

Yea, though I walk through the valley
of the shadow of death,
I will fear no evil;
For You are with me;
Your rod and Your staff, they comfort
me.

You prepare a table before me in the
presence of my enemies;
You anoint my head with oil;
My cup runs over.

*Surely goodness and mercy shall
follow me
All the days of my life;
And I will dwell in the house of the
LORD
Forever.* (Psalm 23)

*For this is God,
Our God forever and ever
He will be our guide
Even to death.* (Psalm 48:14)

*But God will redeem my soul from the power of the grave,
For He shall receive me.* (Psalm 49:15)

*Mark the blameless man, and observe the upright;
For the future of that man is peace.* (Psalm 37:37)

*God is our refuge and strength,
A very present help in trouble.
Therefore, we will not fear,
Even though the earth be removed,
And though the mountains be carried
into the midst of the sea;
Though its waters roar and be troubled,
Though the mountains shake with its swelling.*
(Psalm 46:1-3)

*For the Lord will not cast off forever.
Though He causes grief,
Yet He will show compassion
According to the multitude of His mercies.
For He does not afflict willingly,
Nor grieve the children of men.* (Lamentations 3:31-33)

Through the LORD'S mercies we are not consumed,

Because His compassions fail not.
They are new every morning;
Great is Your faithfulness.
"The LORD is my portion," says my soul,
Therefore I hope in Him! (Lamentations 3:22-24)

I called on Your name, O LORD,
From the lowest pit.
You have heard my voice:
"Do not hide Your ear
From my sighing, from my cry for help."
You drew near on the day I called on You,
And said, Do not fear!" (Lamentations 3:55-57)

Wait on the LORD;
Be of good courage,
And He shall strengthen your heart;
Wait, I say, on the LORD! (Psalm 27:14)

Turn Yourself to me, and have mercy on me,
For I am desolate and afflicted.
The troubles of my heart have enlarged;
Bring me out of my distresses. (Psalm 25:16-17)

I waited patiently for the LORD;
And He inclined to me,
And heard my cry.
He also brought me up out of a horrible pit,
Out of the miry clay,
And set my feet upon a rock,
And established my steps.
He has put a new song in my mouth-
Praise to our God;
Many will see it and fear,
And will trust in the LORD. (Psalm 40:1-3)

The "Prescription of Poetry" lets us see how the children of Israel expressed their emotions during times of suffering, especially during grief. Through this process they could experience God's comfort, grace, and peace.

Personal poems are also helpful in recovering from grief. I am reminded of a poem written by one of our chaplains, Sally Jadlow, for Judie Eby when her mother died. Judie is the wife of Don Eby, CEO of Eby Holdings, Inc., one of Marketplace Ministries' client companies in the Kansas City area. Chaplain Jadlow had developed a relationship with Mary Bickford, Judie's mother, while she was in an assisted living center. The very comforting poem is entitled "Farewell to Mary."

Sweet little Mary with rosebud lips
and twinkling eyes,
who smiled at each one passing by.

With fingers that made beautiful praise
To her loving Lord, most of her days.

With rosy cheeks and snow-white hair,
She always knew when loved-ones were near.

We'll miss you Mary, precious friend,
And look forward to seeing you when this life ends.

Judie Eby and family were so moved by this poem that they framed it with a picture of Mrs. Bickford. It hangs in the corporate office as a reminder of the beautiful life she led. Mrs. Bickford was an accomplished harpist, playing with the Wichita Symphony Orchestra and holding concerts in many churches. Her fingers did indeed make beautiful music to her loving Lord most of her days.

You will not be able to fully experience God's comfort, grace, and peace if you believe you have been wronged, and if you have unsettled issues concerning your loved one's death. The "Prescription of Pardoning" is provided to help you resolve this issue and continue your movement toward full recovery. May you be able to grant a complete pardon, through the working of the Holy Spirit in your life, to anyone you hold a grievance against regarding your loved one's death. Let's examine this important prescription.

PRESCRIPTION OF PARDONING

*Let all bitterness, wrath, anger, clamor, and evil speaking
be put away from you, with all malice.
And be kind to one another, tenderhearted, forgiving one
another, even as God in Christ forgave you.
(Ephesians 4:31-32)*

Often when a loved one dies, unsettled issues remain. These issues often include unresolved anger, poor relationships, and an unsettled grievance or disagreement with the deceased. Too often these issues stop us in the "Readjusting to Reality" process. If not addressed properly, they may cause a number of emotional and physical ailments. We want to provide you with a tool to help you address this critical issue.

Forgiveness is the biblical principle we need to grasp onto to begin the recovery process when this condition exists. To forgive basically means we don't hold a charge against another person, even when the person has wronged us. We call this *pardoning the person* because we will not attempt to get even. True forgiveness is a grace of God and recognizes God's Holy Spirit at work to enable this to truly happen. Since God has forgiven all believers and declared them righteous (justification), He has called us to forgive others when they wrong us. Forgiveness does not mean we forget the wrong or reclassify the wrong as being acceptable. When we forgive another person, we pardon that person and completely release him or her from having to pay for wronging us.

An emotional phase of the grieving process often includes getting angry with the loved one for dying, being angry with God, blaming yourself, blaming the doctors or medical staff, blaming a parent, sibling, or just about anyone. Pardoning the person, or forgiving the person, lets us move to the next step in recovery.

A nurse in a local hospital, Don, said he didn't believe that anyone could ever completely recover from grief. Don based this on his own experience of being raised by an abusive and alcoholic father. While he was growing up, he and his father had never enjoyed the good relationship he desired. After Don became an adult and moved away from home, his father became ill, and they began to try to improve their relationship. They had nearly settled their grievances when his father died.

Although this occurred several years ago, Don still carries the hurt of not completely reconciling with his father. He still carries some anger and bitterness, and although the grief is not as severe as before, he is still grieving over his dad's death.

Regardless of whom you are angry with or blame, living or dead, it is essential for you to forgive that person or those people. We can only really do this through the work of the Holy Spirit in us, because our natural desires are to protect ourselves and put conditions on forgiving or accepting forgiveness. Call upon the Lord in prayer and ask Him to give you the desire and strength, through His grace, to forgive whoever you are angry with or blame for the death of your loved one.

The next prescription, "Prescription of Penmanship," provides ways for you to express your grief. This prescription can also help you release and pardon those you may be angry with or blame for your loved one's death. May you find God's comfort, grace, and peace to be real in your life as you move toward releasing your emotional suffering through the act of penmanship.

PRESCRIPTION OF PENMANSHIP

We are providing this prescription as a tool to help you express your feelings as you experience the swinging phases of grief. Writing in a journal is therapeutic because it lets you express your feelings without judgment or shame. The Psalms are excellent examples of how God's people expressed their pain, emotions, and disappointments.

You will also find this prescription helpful as you express your anger, blame, and disappointment with your loved one's death. If you are angry and blame your loved one who died, use this section to express your feelings and let God enable you to forgive your loved one through the act of journal writing. In your own words, write about the offense with your loved one and why you are angry with his death. Your anger may be caused by your fear of the financial condition and your ability to provide for you and your family. You may be angry because your loved one was your closet friend and you feel abandoned. Maybe you are angry over the way your loved one died, especially if you feel it could have been avoided.

Regardless of the reason, express your true feelings. Ask God to enable you to release this charge against your loved one, and to allow you through His strength, to write a complete release to your loved one. If you are angry or blame someone who is still living, you can also express your feelings through journal writing and forgive that person in the same way, as well as doing it in person.

As you experience the emotional phases of grief, you can also express these feelings by journal writing. Anytime you feel down, discouraged, or upset, simply write these feelings down. It is good to review what you have written over time and observe your emotional changes. May you find the act of journal writing to be an excellent way for you to release your feelings and let the

God of all comfort extend His supernatural grace to you, and give you peace, as you successfully move through the grieving processes.

EXPRESS YOUR EMOTIONAL FEELINGS IN WRITING ON THE FOLLOWING PAGES

PRESCRIPTION OF PICTURES

This prescription is designed to help you remember the happy occasions you experienced with your loved one. If you like, choose pictures for this section that include your shared moments. Remember the good times you shared and thank the Lord for your loved one's life and contributions. We see in Acts 9:36-39 how upon Tabitha's death, her friends reminisced about her deeds of kindness and charity as they showed off the tunics and garments she had made.

At Joppa there was a certain disciple named Tabitha, which is translated Dorcas. This woman was full of good works and charitable deeds which she did.
But it happened in those days that she became sick and died. When they had washed her, they laid her in an upper room. And since Lydda was near Joppa, and the disciples had heard that Peter was there, they sent two men to him, imploring him not to delay in coming to them. Then Peter arose and went with them. When he had come, they brought him to the upper room. And all the widows stood by him weeping, showing the tunics and garments which Dorcas had made while she was with them.

Tabitha's friends remembered her life in their moments of grief. This prescription will help you if you can do the same thing. During the quiet moments of the day, or when the Lord brings your loved one to mind, simply open your copy of *The Christian Comfort Companion* and reminisce. Although it is good to reminisce, make sure you don't use the pictures as idols of worship, which could keep you anchored in the "Resistance to Reality" process of grief, and make you unable to successfully readjust to the reality of your loved one's death.

77

As I shared the concept of this book with my pastor, Dr. Vic Borden of Red Bridge Baptist Church, and mentioned the "Prescription of Pictures" section, he pulled out his wallet and showed me the pictures of his two siblings and dad who were killed in an automobile accident years ago. He keeps these pictures with him and has found them to be especially comforting.

May the pictures you choose for this section give you precious moments of reflection as you thank God for His comfort, grace, and peace in enabling you to proceed in the grief recovery processes. **Place your selected photos and documents on the acid-free photo paper provided in the back of the book.**

PRESCRIPTION OF PERIODIC RECONCILIATION

At certain times of the year you will be especially reminded of your loved one. You may find these times to be the most difficult for you in experiencing grief. These might include your loved one's birthday; your anniversary; holidays such as Christmas, Easter, Thanksgiving; family reunions; annual functions; and other occasions. During these times you will find this prescription to be extremely helpful.

First, accept the fact that because your loved one is now gone, these events and days will be different for you. If you try to keep things unchanged and make the same arrangements as if your deceased loved one were present, you may have a much harder time readjusting to this new reality. We have defined this as "Prescription of Periodic Reconciliation" because each year you will need to accept this new reality. It may cause you to modify a family tradition to adjust for your loved one's absence. For instance, instead of cooking a big family meal for Christmas, Thanksgiving or Easter, you may wish to have dinner with a child, sibling, other relative, or friend.

On your loved one's birthday, you may choose to do something particularly meaningful to you. Be innovative with another relative, church member, or friend, and arrange in advance to do something you would really enjoy doing. On these occasions, you really need to be with others, and resist staying alone at home or spending time by yourself. You may choose a friend who has walked with you through the grieving processes. The main focus should be to accept the changed state of your life and make necessary adjustments to live with the new reality.

Secondly and most important, let God switch your heart and mind from an earthly perspective to a heavenly perspective. If your loved one knew Christ, he or she is in heaven, in the presence of our Lord and Savior, Jesus

Christ. The Apostle Paul reminds us in 2 Corinthians 5:6-8, that when a believer dies, the immaterial part of the person (soul and spirit) separates from the body and goes immediately into God's presence:

So we are always confident, knowing that
while we are at home in the body we are absent
from the Lord. For we walk by faith, not by
sight. We are confident, yes, well pleased rather
to be absent from the body and to be present with the Lord.

The Apostle Paul was confident about what happens to the soul and spirit of believers who die. Therefore, we should rejoice about the perfect state of existence that our loved one is experiencing. It may take some time before you will be able to honestly say you are pleased that your loved one is in God's presence, rather than with you.

The earthly perspective focuses on our suffering, and celebrating without our loved one. However, when we switch to a heavenly scene and see from our loved one's perspective, we see a stark contrast between what we are experiencing and what our loved one is experiencing.

Psalm 16:11 gives us insight:

You will show me the path of life;
In your presence is fullness of joy;
At Your right hand are pleasures forevermore.

We see that those who placed their faith in Jesus Christ are in God's presence when they die, where they are experiencing fullness of joy and eternal life. They are not lacking anything. Instead, they are rejoicing and experiencing exceeding gladness. It is more than we can even imagine. In addition, Christ is on the right hand of

God, which is a figurative way of explaining Christ's position of authority. Therefore, our loved ones have the pleasure of reigning with Christ forever. Our minds cannot fully grasp the magnitude of heaven because of its glory and perfection. The Apostle Paul glimpsed heaven and could not find the words to adequately describe its glory. Let's look at what he said about what God enabled him to experience.

> *It is doubtless not profitable for me to boast. I will*
> *come to visions and revelations of the Lord.*
> *I know a man in Christ who fourteen years ago-*
> *whether in the body I do not know,*
> *or whether out of the body I do not know,*
> *God knows-such a one was caught up to the third heaven.*
> *And I know such a man-whether in the body*
> *or out of the body I do not know, God knows-*
> *how he was caught up into Paradise and heard*
> *inexpressible words, which it is not*
> *lawful for a man to utter* (2 Corinthians 12:1-4).

Paul seems reluctant and humbled in trying to explain his experience probably because he wanted to share it without boasting. Therefore, he tells about his experience in the context of a man in Christ who had the experience. We know he was talking about himself because he explains that God gave him a thorn in the flesh to keep him humble because he had received a glimpse of the third heaven (paradise). Paul prayed for God to remove the thorn, but He did not. He stated that His grace was sufficient for Paul (2 Corinthians 12:7-9). Paul was not sure if his experience was in the body or out of the body. However, he did know that what he heard and probably saw was inexpressible for man. Most likely, Paul heard the worship and praise of God around the throne by believers who had died and angels, as the Apostle John experienced in His vision (Revelation 4-5).

Those who are in God's presence have attained a perfection of holiness we can only imagine. I am convinced they have no desire to return to earth, to live in a sinful, corrupt world. However, in our humanity, we will certainly miss them. At precious moments a certain scent, specific words, scenes, or certain people may especially remind you of your loved one. This may cause the hurt to resurface and make you miss your loved one. It is perfectly acceptable to acknowledge that you miss your loved one, and you may choose to write your feelings in the "Prescription of Penmanship." You can also spend time in prayer, asking God to give you a special measure of His grace to help you through this.

On special yearly occasions, I receive a special grace of comfort from God by reflecting on my loved ones being in God's presence and no longer suffering. God uses this perspective to give me a special sense of his comfort, grace, and peace. He will give this to you, too.

PRESCRIPTION OF PHYSICAL CARE

When we experience grief and our emotions suffer, we may also suffer physically. We must be careful to recognize the effects of grief on our physical condition. When we are grieving, we tend to focus on the loss of our loved one, and may stop taking care of our bodies. A grieving person may lose his or her appetite, may lose the desire to get up, and may find it difficult to resume normal activities. In some cases, rather than not having an appetite, one may gain weight by eating excessively.

The Apostle John gives us insight into the importance of caring for not only our souls but also for our bodies. In 3 John 2, John tells Gaius how he prays for him.

Beloved, I pray that you may prosper in all things and be in health, just as your soul prospers.

John's prayer was for Gaius to prosper in all things including physical health, just as he has prospered spiritually in truth. He is not praying with the belief that the elder will never get sick, and will live forever. We will not always experience good health. However, we should strive to enhance our spiritual, emotional, and physical health — especially during grief — to glorify God as we go through the grief recovery processes.

To maintain good health during grief, you may choose to exercise by walking in the neighborhood, joining a health club, riding a bike, or doing aerobics. You will not want to do much during the initial phases of grief, but it is important for you to do small things to care for your body.

When our daughter, Kathleen, experienced the stillbirth of Baby J, her church, Canaan Christian Fellowship, encouraged her to take care of her body. The church gave her a basket loaded with lotion, perfume, hair preparation, a certificate to the beauty parlor, and other items.

Exercise and being in good physical condition helps us emotionally. Caring for our bodies will help heal our emotional suffering, especially during grief. During grief some people suffer a low self esteem and lose confidence in themselves. Do small things such as going to the beauty shop or spa, shopping, swimming, bowling, playing golf or tennis, or doing any activity that will help you begin to move on toward "readjusting to reality."

You may choose to take lessons in an activity that will relieve your mind from focusing on the loss of your loved one. Feel free to be innovative and to do things you may have always longed to do. The main thing is to try to do something of a physical nature to help you begin to recover. Ask a relative, friend, or partner who is walking with you through grief recovery to help you follow through even though you may not feel like doing anything. May you begin to take care of your body and make the necessary adjustments to help you move through the grief recovery processes.

PRESCRIPTION OF PLEASURES

The twelfth and final prescription to help you recover from grief is that of enjoying life again with renewed hope and peace about your loved one's death. The "Prescription of Pleasures" is fully realized when you reach the "Reattaining Reality" process, but it may also help as you begin to readjust to living without your loved one.

One of the wisest men to ever live gave us insight into how to enjoy a meaningful life. Solomon, David's son, wrote Ecclesiastes, which addresses the futility of worldly pleasures and possessions. He found all worldly pleasures and possessions apart from God to be totally empty and unfulfilling. We are not suggesting that you engage in pleasures and possessions without regarding God, but begin to enjoy life again in accordance with godly principles and convictions.

Solomon wrote in Ecclesiastes 5:18-19:

Here is what I have seen. It is good and
fitting for one to eat and drink, and to enjoy
the good of all his labor in which he toils
under the sun all the days of his life which
God gives him; for it is his heritage.
As for every man to whom God has
given riches and wealth and given him
power to eat of it, to receive his heritage
and rejoice in his labor-this is the gift of God.

Solomon acknowledges that the pleasures and riches from work are gifts from God and are our heritage from Him. We are to enjoy life again in this context. We can begin to enjoy the product of our labor again. The pleasures include doing things that bring you joy, satisfaction, and spiritual enhancement. If your spouse died, you may feel free to date again and possibly remarry.

In other cases, it may simply mean that you are able to enjoy church functions, the opera, sporting events, vacation, or things that are meaningful to you.

Initially, you may find doing pleasurable things difficult, and you may feel guilty. But continue to work through the other prescriptions until you begin to experience God's comfort, grace, and peace, letting you enjoy life again with renewed hope and peace.

Solomon ended Ecclesiastes with these words in 12:13-14:

Let us hear the conclusion of the whole matter:
"Fear God and keep His commandments,
for this is man's all.
For God will bring every work into judgment,
Including every secret thing,
Whether good or evil."

We are to enjoy God's gifts with reverence to Him, and to be obedient to His Word. The reason we are to do this is because of our accountability to God in how we live. We will all appear before God, and therefore, we should enjoy the pleasures of life, but in reverence to God. May you enjoy the pleasures of life again as you glorify God through your reverence and obedience to Him.

POSTLUDE OF GRIEF

Grief does not follow a set pattern. The phases of grief can cause you to experience all kinds of difficulties and despair. However, the purpose of this book is to direct your attention to the Source of all hope, our Lord and Savior, Jesus Christ. Through His comfort, grace, and peace you will overcome grief and be able to hope again. We sincerely pray that you have been comforted through a better understanding of the grief processes and by applying the twelve prescriptions of grief recovery. We want to encourage you to apply all twelve grief recovery prescriptions to your life. Full recovery is not quickly or easily achieved because of the emotional phases of grief. However, we found these twelve prescriptions to be helpful in enabling us to experience God's comfort, grace, and peace.

Your emotional phases of grief will be like a roller coaster ride. I grew up in Dallas, Tex., and as a child, one of my most exciting experiences was going to the Texas State Fair. I remember one year especially, when I was about eleven years old and went to the fair with my two older sisters, Mary and Olivia, and some neighborhood kids.

During that time, in the Midway, (the big amusement park area of the fair grounds) was a gigantic wooden roller coaster, called the Lightning. I had never ridden the Lightning before, but my older sisters persuaded me to ride it. I will never forget my fear as I stepped into the ride's car and was locked in with a shoulder and waist harness. As the car slowly climbed to the first big peak, Mary and Olivia held their hands straight up and called for everyone else to do the same. Not knowing any better, I also held my hands up.

The car continued to move ... clank, clank, clank, clank ... until it reached the top of the hill. Then the bottom of my world seemed to fall completely out, as I experienced the gravitational pull back to earth and back to reality. I held on to the bar in front of me for dear life as the car zoomed up and down and around the curves. My hands became sweaty as I clutched the bar.

As I recall that experience, I realize it wasn't my holding on to the bar that kept me safely in the car, but the shoulder and waist harness. That was the first and last time I rode the Lightning.

The phases of grief are like riding the Lightning. You don't know what your experience will be like until you undergo it. Some days will be almost unbearable as your emotions swing up and down and around, as if you're emotionally riding the Lightning. But God is like the shoulder and waist harness that keeps us locked safely in. Actually, He is infinitely better. God, through His comfort, grace, and peace will enable you to safely ride through grief processes. He has you securely locked in and will bring you safely through.

No one knows completely all aspects of grief or how each person will respond during grief. This book cannot possibly cover all of your experiences. Each experience of grief may be different. Today, we have many super roller coasters at many amusement parks all over the United States. The roller coasters in these parks do much more than what the Lightning did — they carry you upside down and around. Your next grief experience may be different than your previous experience, but be assured that God is unchangeable. He will still keep you safe and secure and carry you through the processes even though it may seem as if you are on a super roller coaster.

This book has been primarily written to comfort believers whose loved ones were also believers in Jesus Christ. If you are not sure of your loved one's spiritual condition at death, be encouraged that no one but God knows a person's heart. Your loved one could have made a death-bed profession of faith in Jesus Christ, similar to that of the thief on the cross (Luke 23:40-43). Although his life might not have clearly indicated a walk with Christ, his profession of faith as a child could have been sincere and accepted by God for eternity. You must leave that up to our loving and just God because you can do nothing about it now.

However, there is something you can do now regarding your own relationship with the Lord. I want to encourage you to be sure that your own relationship with Christ is secure. We don't know God's ways or thoughts, but your loved one's death can glorify God if you or a family member come to a closer walk with Jesus Christ as a result of the death. If you have any doubts, you can settle this by making a personal profession of faith in Jesus Christ, by repenting and believing in Him with all your heart.

Here are some paraphrased scriptural facts to help you place your faith and trust in Jesus Christ now.

- *You, like everyone, have sinned against a holy God. Before having a personal relationship with Him, you have chosen to go your own way. In doing so, you have fallen short of God's standard for your life, which is sin. (Romans 3:23)*

- *Since God is holy and just, there must be a payment for the sin you have committed and that payment is death. You will die both physically and spiritually. Spiritual death is being eternally separated from God. (Romans 6:23)*

- *Motivated by His love for you, God has provided a gift of eternal life for you by offering you a personal relationship with His Son, Jesus Christ. (Romans 6:23)*

- *God has proven His love for you by the fact that although you have continued to sin against Him, if you place your trust and faith in Jesus Christ, God will accept Christ's death as sufficient payment for your sins. (Romans 5:8)*

- *You must recognize that there is nothing you can do — regardless of who you are or how much good to society you have done — that will gain you favor with God. You cannot set the rules. Since God is your Creator, He has set the rules about the requirements for entering heaven. You must accept God's grace through faith and trust in Jesus Christ to be forgiven of your sins and be made right with God. (Ephesians 2:8-9)*

- *You must humbly come before God in prayer, confessing to Him that through His strength, you are renouncing your old way of life and are committing to live under the Lordship and authority of Jesus Christ. You must believe that Jesus Christ not only died for your sins, but God raised Him from the dead, proving to the world that His death paid the penalty for sin. (Romans 10:9)*

- *You must be open to God's Spirit working in you to change you and conform you into Christ's image. (2 Corinthians 5:17)*

If you aren't sure of your salvation, won't you get that point settled between you and God today? Won't you humbly go before God in prayer at this time and commit your life to Christ through confessing your sins, through offering a repentant heart, and through sincerely asking Christ to come into your heart and save you right now?

Writing this book has been a long journey, and we give all praise and glory to our Lord and Savior, Jesus Christ, for any benefits that result from it. Our purpose and sincere desire is that your working through this book will result in a closer walk with the Lord. We commit to pray regularly that the readers of this book will successfully go through the grief processes and personally experience God's comfort, grace, and peace. May you now look to the future with renewed hope and faith in Jesus Christ.

ADDITIONAL RESOURCES

Kolf, June C., *When Will I Stop Hurting?* (Grand Rapids: Baker Book House, 1987).

Lewis, C. S., *A Grief Observed* (New York: Bantam Books, 1976).

Mayfield, James L., *Discovering Grace in Grief* (Nashville: Upper Room Books, 1994).

Sittser, Gerald L., *A Grace Disguised* (Grand Rapids: Zondervan Publishing House, 1995).

Westberg Granger E., *Good Grief* (Minneapolis: Fortress Press, 1971).

ABOUT THE AUTHORS

Rev. Maceo Gray and his wife of 45 years, Annie (Ann) P. Gray, are 1998 honors and high honors graduates, respectively, of Dallas Theological Seminary. Rev. Gray received the four year Master of Theology degree and Ann Gray received the Master of Arts in Cross-Cultural Ministries degree. She was also certified by the seminary to teach English as a Second Language. During graduation, Rev. Gray received "The W. E. Hawkins Jr. Award in Christian Service" and "The Lewis Sperry Chafer Award,"named after the founder and first president of Dallas Theological Seminary. Ann Gray received "The Fredrik Franson Award in World Missions."

The Grays reside in Kansas City, MO and are the proud parents of two grown daughters, Karen L. Selby, wife of Major Christopher Selby (USAF), and Kathleen A. Smith, wife of Todd H. Smith. Their five grandchildren, Charity Selby, Christopher Selby, Jr., Jessica K. Smith, Joshua T. Smith, and Jayna A. Smith are the joy of their lives.

The Grays took early retirement in 1993 from their corporate positions to answer God's call to full-time ministry. Rev. Gray worked thirty years for AlliedSignal Corporation in Kansas City, MO., retiring as an Engineering Program Manager. Ann Gray worked twenty years for Pfizer Corporation in Lee's Summit, MO., retiring as a Senior Microbiologist/Chemist.

Rev. Gray is a native of Dallas, Tex. Besides his seminary degree, he holds the Bachelor of Science in Electrical Engineering degree from Prairie View A. & M. University, the Master of Science in Electrical Engineering degree from the University of Missouri, and the Executive Fellows MBA degree from Rockhurst College. For the past fourteen years, he has served as a chaplain and in several management positions for Marketplace Ministries, a nation-wide corporate chaplaincy ministry with headquarters in Dallas. He received the Chaplain of the Year Award in 1997. He is currently the Midwest Region Vice President responsible for the ministry in Missouri, Kansas, Oklahoma, Nebraska, Colorado, New Mexico, South Dakota, North Dakota, Utah, and Wyoming.

Ann Gray is a native of Fairfield, Tex. Besides her seminary degree, she holds the Bachelor of Science degree in Microbiology from the University of Missouri at Kansas City. She has taught English as a Second Language to international students at El Centro Community College in Dallas, and Johnson County Community College in Overland Park, Kansas.

Rev. Gray is licensed and ordained to the gospel ministry by Red Bridge Baptist Church where the Grays have served for 32 years. The Grays would like to hear from you. Please e-mail (maceo.gray@sbcglobal.net) them your comments about this book.

To order additional copies of

The Christian Comfort Companion

send $12.95* plus $2.00 shipping and handling to:

Hope Again Ministries Publishing
P. O. Box 481331
Kansas City, MO 64148
(816) 718-4441
maceo.gray@sbcglobal.net

*Quantity discounts available

**Churches, funeral homes and other institutions
may have their personalized
message and photo printed on the entire back
cover of the book in quantities
of 10 or more. Ideal to give as a complimentary
aid to grief recovery.**

PLACE YOUR SELECTED PHOTOS AND DOCUMENTS ON THE FOLLOWING PAGES!

(USE PHOTO MOUNTING TAPE OR GLUE TO PLACE ITEMS ON THE ACID-FREE PHOTO PAPER).